SCIENCE KIDS
Colors

PURPLE

Jared Siemens

www.av2books.com

LET'S READ AV² BY WEIGL™
ADDED VALUE • AUDIO VISUAL

Go to **www.av2books.com**, and enter this book's unique code.

BOOK CODE

P456565

AV² by Weigl brings you media enhanced books that support active learning.

AV² provides enriched content that supplements and complements this book. Weigl's AV² books strive to create inspired learning and engage young minds in a total learning experience.

Your AV² Media Enhanced books come alive with...

Audio
Listen to sections of the book read aloud.

Video
Watch informative video clips.

Embedded Weblinks
Gain additional information for research.

Try This!
Complete activities and hands-on experiments.

Key Words
Study vocabulary, and complete a matching word activity.

Quizzes
Test your knowledge.

Slide Show
View images and captions, and prepare a presentation.

... and much, much more!

Published by AV² by Weigl
350 5th Avenue, 59th Floor New York, NY 10118
Websites: www.av2books.com   www.weigl.com

Library of Congress Control Number: 2014934863

ISBN 978-1-4896-1258-8 (hardcover)
ISBN 978-1-4896-1259-5 (softcover)
ISBN 978-1-4896-1260-1 (single user eBook)
ISBN 978-1-4896-1261-8 (multi-user eBook)

Printed in the United States of America in North Mankato, Minnesota
1 2 3 4 5 6 7 8 9 0 18 17 16 15 14

042014
WEP150314

Project Coordinator: Aaron Carr
Designer: Mandy Christiansen

Weigl acknowledges Getty Images and iStock as the primary image suppliers for this title.

SCIENCE KIDS
Colors

PURPLE

CONTENTS

3

What is this color
I see all around?

It's purple I see!
Where can purple be found?

I see
a purple blanket.

I see a pillow
for your head.

What other purple things can you find near your bed?

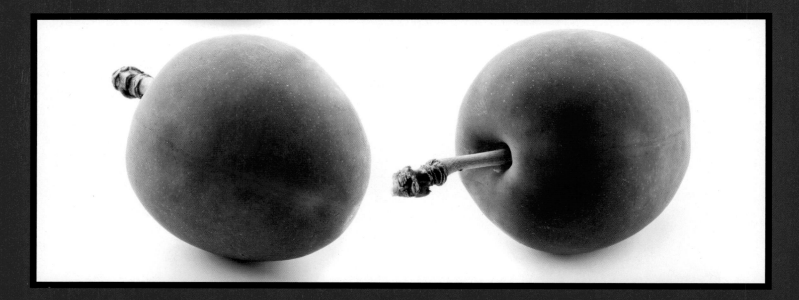

Purple plums and eggplants are healthy foods to eat.

Do you know a purple food that is a tasty treat?

I see
a purple puzzle.

I see
a teddy bear.

Do you see other purple toys?
Can you tell me where?

11

Are there purple things outside? Can you name them all?

I see purple flowers growing on a wall.

I see
a purple starfish.

I see
an insect, too.

Are there any purple animals
that live close to you?

Is purple at the playground?
Purple slides are grand.

I see a purple shovel and bucket in the sand.

I see
purple scissors.

I see a purple
number three.

Do you see purple at school? Where else could it be?

Purple can mean springtime when flowers bloom and grow.

I found purple eggs at Easter.
Can you put them in a row?

Find where these purple things belong in this book.

Go back through the pages and have a close look!

KEY WORDS

Research has shown that as much as 65 percent of all written material published in English is made up of 300 words. These 300 words cannot be taught using pictures or learned by sounding them out. They must be recognized by sight. This book contains 60 common sight words to help young readers improve their reading fluency and comprehension. This book also teaches young readers several important content words, such as proper nouns. These words are paired with pictures to aid in learning and improve understanding.

Page	Sight Words First Appearance	Page	Content Words First Appearance
4	all, around, I, is, see, this, what	4	color
5	be, can, found, it's, where	5	purple
6	a, for, head, your	6	blanket, pillow
7	find, near, other, things, you	7	bed
8	and, are, eat, foods, to	8	eggplants, plums
9	do, know, that	9	treat
11	me, tell	10	puzzle, teddy bear
12	there, name, them	11	toys
13	on	12	outside
14	an, too	13	flowers, wall
15	animals, any, close, live	14	insect, starfish
16	at, the	16	playground, slides
17	in	17	bucket, sand, shovel
18	number	18	scissors
19	could, it, school	20	springtime
20	grow, mean, when	21	Easter, eggs, row
21	put		
22	book, these		
23	back, go, have, look, pages, through		

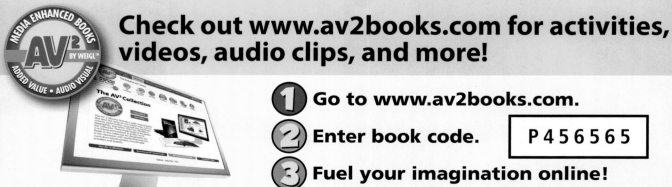

Check out www.av2books.com for activities, videos, audio clips, and more!

1 Go to www.av2books.com.

2 Enter book code. P456565

3 Fuel your imagination online!

www.av2books.com

24